Air Fryer

Seafood Cookbook

Delicious Seafood Recipes Book

Sandy Wells

Table of Contents

What Is Air Frying?

First, a quick explanation of what air frying is and isn't. They don't fry food at all. They are more like a self-contained convection oven than a deep fat fryer. Most units have one or more heating elements, along with a fan or two to circulate the hot air. These appliances quickly heat and circulate the hot air around and through the food in the tray. This cooking method takes advantage of the heat and the drying effect of the air to cook foods quickly, leaving them crisp and browned on the outside but still moist inside. While the results can be similar to using a deep fryer, they are not identical.

What Are The Pros And Cons Of An Air Fryer?

While the enthusiasm about these products may be a bit overblown, there are some solid benefits to using an air fryer, as well as some major downsides.

Pros Of An Air Fryer

1. Healthier Meals

You do not need to use much (or any) oil in these appliances to get your food crispy and browned! Most users just spritz a little oil on the item and then proceed to the cooking cycle. The hot air takes advantage of the little bit of oil, and any excess oil just drains away from the food. This makes these devices ideal for making fresh and frozen fries, onion rings, mozzarella sticks, chicken wings, and nuggets. Unlike a traditional oven, air frying items are cooked faster and the excess oil doesn't soak into your food. So the claims that they use less oil and make healthier meals are true!

2. Quicker, More Efficient Cooking

Air fryers take just minutes to preheat, and most of the heat stays inside the appliance. Foods cook faster than in an oven or on a stovetop because this heat is not lost to the surrounding air. Even frozen foods are quickly cooked because the effect of the heat is intensified by the circulating air. These units are also more energy-efficient than an oven. Using a fryer will not heat your house in the summer, and the cost of the electricity used is just pennies. Since the cooking cycle is also shorter, you can see that using a fryer makes most cooking faster and more efficient than traditional appliances!

3. Versatility

You can use them to air fry, stir fry, reheat, bake, broil, roast, grill, steam, and even rotisserie in some models. Besides the fries and nuggets, you can make hot dogs and sausages, steak, chicken breasts or thighs, grilled sandwiches, stir-fried meats and veggies, roasted or steamed veggies, all kinds of fish and shrimp dishes, even cakes and desserts. If your unit is large enough, you can even bake a whole chicken or small turkey, or do a beef or pork roast. They are more than just a fryer!

4. Space-Saving

Most units are about the size of a coffee maker. Some models are small and super-compact, making them perfect for small kitchens, kitchenettes, dorm rooms, or RVs. An air fryer can replace an oven in a situation that lacks one and can be more useful than a toaster oven or steamer. If you use it frequently you will likely be happy to give it a home on your kitchen counter!

5. Easy To Use

Most fryers are designed to be easy to use. Just set the cooking temperature and time, put your food in the basket, and walk away. Of course, you will get better results if you shake your food once or twice during the cooking cycle, especially for things like fries, chips, wings, and nuggets. This ensures even browning and perfect results. Many air fryer enthusiasts have even taught their children to use them for making after school snacks or quick lunches!

Cons of an Air Fryer

1. Quality Issues

Air fryers are mostly made from plastic and inexpensive metal parts. They may or may not bear up after months or years of use. The heating elements, controls, and fans tend to go out eventually, and once they do your unit is useless. The metal cooking baskets and pans do not tend to last very long and often need to be replaced. Print on the dials or control panels can wear off. Even expensive units can have these issues, and some brands seem to have a lot of reported problems. These are not sturdy, long-lasting kitchen appliances overall.

2. Takes Up Space

Ok, I had "Space Saver" listed as a pro...how can it be a con as well? Easy! They do take up space, either on your counter or stored away in a cabinet. If you use it frequently this might not be a problem...but if you only drag it out to make the occasional batch of wings then the loss of space might not make it worth it to you. It depends on how and if you use it. Some units are fairly heavy as well, and might not be very easy to move around. They have the potential to be just another appliance you use a few times and then sell at a yard sale.

3. Not Ideal For Large Families

You will see some fryers advertised for "large families" but what does that mean? Most air fryers are best suited to making food for 1-4 people (depending on the capacity). There are very few that can handle making food for more than 4, and they often still require cooking in batches. For large families, a true convection air frying oven would probably be a better choice.

A medium-sized fryer with a capacity of 3.5 quarts can usually handle the main dish for two or a main and side dish for one. A large unit with a capacity of 5.8 quarts can handle the main dish like a whole chicken...which theoretically means enough to serve 4 people, as long as you cook the rest of the food in another appliance. So these are ideal for smaller families or single users, or a dorm or office snack maker.

4. Learning Curve

They ARE easy to use, but there is still a learning curve. Each unit has its peculiarities that you will have to figure out. They come with cooking guides and recipes, but those are more recommendations rather than firm instructions. It may take a few trials before you get the results that you want. Luckily the internet is filled with users who have shared their experiences, so finding tips is pretty easy.

1. Tuna Patties Servings

Time: 50 minutes

Ingredients:

- 5 oz. of canned tuna
- 1 tsp. lime juice
- 1 tsp. paprika
- ¼ cup flour
- ½ cup milk
- 1 small onion, diced

- 2 eggs
- 1 tsp. chili powder, optional
- ½ tsp. salt

Instructions:

Place all of the **Ingredients** in a bowl and mix well to combine. Make two large patties, or a few smaller ones, out of the mixture.Place them on a lined sheet and refrigerate for 30 minutes.Preheat the air fryer to 350 degrees F. Air fry the patties for about 6 minutes on each side.

Nutrition Facts

Calories 235.5, Carbohydrates 20.5 g, Fat 6.6 g, Protein 24.6 g

2. Air Fried Calamari and Tomato Pasta

Preparation time: 25mins

Ingredients

- 2 cloves garlic, minced
- 1 lb. sliced calamari, cut into rings
- 1 egg 1 cup Italian bread crumbs
- 1 tbsp. of olive oil
- ½ cup diced onion
- 2 tsps. Italian seasoning
- 2 (15 oz.) cans diced tomatoes, drained
- 1 lb. dry angel hair pasta
- ½ cup grated parmesan

Instructions

- Preheat fryer to 360 degrees.
- Dip the calamari into the egg and then into the breadcrumbs. Coating all sides. Place in the air fryer basket and drizzle with olive oil. Cook for 15 minutes. Meanwhile, bring a large pot of water to a boil.
- Add the pasta and cook for 10 minutes or until tender. Drain. Combine the pasta, garlic, onion, Italian seasoning, and diced tomatoes. Heat just until hot. Spoon on to a serving plate. Remove calamari from air fryer and place on top of pasta. Sprinkle with Parmesan

Nutrition facts:

Calorie 303.6 Fats 14.2g Fiber 0.06g Carbs 28.3g Protein 18.7g

3. Pistachio Crusted Salmon

Prep Time: 15 - 20 minutes

Ingredients:

- 1 salmon fillet
- 1 tsp. mustard
- 3 tbsp. pistachios
- Pinch of sea salt
- Pinch of garlic powder
- Pinch of black pepper
- 1 tsp. lemon juice1 tsp. grated Parmesan cheese1 tsp. olive oil

Instructions:

Preheat the air fryer to 350 degrees F.Whisk the mustard and lemon juice together.Season the salmon with salt, pepper, and garlic powder.Brush the olive oil on all sides.Brush the mustard/lemon mixture on top of the salmon.Chop the pistachios finely and combine them with the Parmesan cheese.Sprinkle them on top of the salmon.Place the salmon in the air fryer basket with the skin side down.Cook for about 10 minutes, or to your liking.

Nutrition Facts

Calories 357, Carbohydrates 8.2 g, Fat 23.8 g, Protein 28.8 g

4. Pecan Crusted Salmon

Preparation time: 20mins

Ingredients

- ½ cup pecans
- 3 tbsp. fresh chopped parsley
- 1 tsp. salt
- ½ tsp. ground black pepper
- 3 tbsp. Dijon mustard
- 3 tbsp. olive oil
- 1 tbsp. honey
- ½ cup Panko breadcrumbs
- 4 salmon filets 1 tbsp. lemon juice

Instructions

- Preheat air fryer to 390 degrees F.

- In a small bowl combine the mustard, oil, and honey. Combine the Panko, pecans, parsley, salt, and pepper in a food processor and process until crumbs are fine.
- Dip the salmon in the mustard mixture then dip the salmon into the pecan mixture, pressing the pecans into all sides of the fish.
- Place the coated salmon in the fryer basket and cook for 10 minutes.
- Drizzle with lemon juice.

Nutrition facts:

Calorie 353.2

Fats 24.8g

Fiber 1.1g

Carbs 1.7g

Protein 30.5g

5. Broiled Tilapia Done

Preparation time: 9mins

Ingredients

- 1 to 1 1/2 lb. tilapia fillets
- molly mcbutter or butter buds
- light spritz of canola oil from an oil spritzer
- Old Bay seasoning,
- lemon pepper
- salt

Instructions

- Thaw fillets, if frozen. Spray the basket of your air fryer with cooking spray.
- Place fillets in the basket (do not stack them) and season to taste with the spices. Spray lightly with oil.
- Set temperature at 400 degrees and set timer for 7 minutes.
- When the timer goes off, check for doneness. Fish should flake easily with a fork.
- Serve and enjoy with your favorite veggies.

Nutrition facts:

Calorie 110

Fats 3g

Fiber 0g

Carbs 23g

6. Prawn Curry

Preparation time: 15mins

Ingredients

- 2 tbsp. curry powder
- 1 medium finely chopped onion
- 1½ cup chicken broth
- ½ tsp. of coriander
- 6 king prawns
- 1 tsp. salt

- ½ tsp. ground black pepper
- 1 tbsp. olive oil
- 1 tbsp. tomato paste

Instructions

Preheat the air fryer to 370 degrees F. Season the prawns with salt and pepper.

Cook for 7 minutes. Meanwhile, heat the olive oil in a large skillet. Once hot add the onion.

Cook until soft. Sit in the curry, tomato paste, and coriander.

Cook, stirring, for 1 minute.

Add the chicken broth and stir until smooth.

Remove prawns from the fryer and add to the sauce.

Nutrition facts:

Calorie 294.2 Fats 11g Fiber 7.4g Carbs 21.4g

7. Crusted Halibut

Preparation time: 30mins

Ingredients

- 2 tsp. lemon zest
- 1 tsp. salt
- ½ tsp. ground black pepper
- ¾ cup Panko bread crumbs
- ½ cup fresh parsley, chopped
- ¼ cup fresh dill, chopped
- 4 halibut filets
- 1 tbsp. olive oil

Instructions

- Preheat the air fryer to 390 degrees F.
- Combine all **Ingredients** except halibut and olive oil in a food processor and pulse until the mixture is a fine crumb.
- gently coat the halibut in the mixture and place inside the fryer basket.
- Drizzle with olive oil and cook for 25 minutes.

Nutrition facts:

Calorie 454

Fats 15g

Fiber 5g

Carbs 38g

Protein 4g

8. Shrimp and Mushroom Risotto

Preparation time: 30mins

Ingredients

- 4 Chicken Legs
- 2 tbsp. Olive Oil
- 4 tsp. dried Basil
- 2 tsp. minced garlic
- Pinch of Pepper
- Pinch of Salt

- 1 Lemon, sliced

Instructions

- Preheat your Air Fryer to 350 degrees F.
- Brush the chicken with the oil and sprinkle with the remaining **Ingredients**.
- Place in the Air Fryer and arrange the lemon slices around the chicken legs.
- Close the lid and cook for 20 minutes.

Nutrition facts:

Calorie 328.3

Fats 14.5g

Fiber 2.3g

Carbs 24.1g

Protein 24.4g

9. Halibut Sitka

Preparation time: 20mins

Ingredients

- ½ cup green onion, chopped
- ½ cup mayonnaise
- ½ cup sour cream
- 6 (8 oz.) skinless halibut filets
- 1 tsp. salt
- ½ tsp. ground black pepper
- 1 tsp. dry dill

Instructions

- Preheat the air fryer to 390 degrees F
- Season the halibut with salt and pepper, place on the fryer plate.
- In a small bowl, combine the remaining **Ingredients**.
- Mix well then spread over the top of the halibut. Cook for 15 minutes.

!

Nutrition facts:

Calorie 333.26

Fats 37.03g

Fiber 0.06g

Carbs 1.74g

Protein 22.17g

10. Air Fried Cod Nuggets

Total Time: 15 Minutes

Ingredients

- 1 lb cod
- 1/4 cup all-purpose flour
- 1/2 tsp salt
- 1/2 tsp black pepper
- 2 egg
- 1 cup breadcrumbs panko
- 1 tsp garlic powder
- 6 oz Greek yogurt plain
- 2 Tbsp dill fresh, chopped
- 1 lemon juiced

Instructions

- Cut cod into 1-inch pieces.
- In a shallow dish, combine flour, salt, and pepper. In a second dish, whisk the 2 eggs. In a third dish, combine panko and garlic powder.
- Set the air fryer to 400° F.
- It takes 3 steps to properly bread the codpieces. First, coat the codpieces with the flour mixture. For the second coat, dip it in the eggs. For the final and coat, cover it with the panko mixture.
- Once all of your pieces are coated, cook in the air fryer for 10-12 minutes, flipping halfway through.
- While cod is cooking, whisk together yogurt, dill, and lemon juice.
- Serve cod immediately with yogurt sauce.

Nutrition

- Carbohydrates: 17g | Protein: 24g | Fat: 5g | Sodium: 862mg | Potassium: 97mg | Fiber: 1g

11. Air Fryer Bacon Wrapped Shrimp

Prep Time: 5 Minutes

Cook Time: 10 Minutes

Total Time: 15 Minutes

Ingredients

- 1 pound raw shrimp (peeled with tails on)
- 1 pound bacon (12 slices cut in half)
- 1 jalapeño pepper (seeded and cut into thin strips)
- 1 cup cocktail sauce
- 1/4 cup chipotle peppers in adobo sauce (chopped fine)

Instructions

- Preheat the air fryer at 390F for 5 minutes while you prep the shrimp.
- Wrap the shrimp
- Cut your bacon slices in half.
- If you haven't already, slice the jalapeño thin.
- Peel the shrimp leaving the tail end on if you want to.
- Place a shrimp and a thin slice of jalapeño on one end of the shrimp.
- Roll the shrimp in the bacon wrapping it tightly.
- Chill the shrimp for 10-15 minutes to set the bacon.
- Make the chipotle cocktail dipping sauce
- Mix the cocktail sauce and the chopped chipotle peppers.
- Chill until ready to serve with the bacon-wrapped shrimp.

Air Fry The Shrimp

- Air Fry the shrimp by placing them in the air fryer basket.
- Don't crowd them and make sure there is space between them so the bacon can crisp and the pieces don't stick together.
- Fry for 5 minutes at 390F.
- Flip the shrimp and air fry for another 4-5 minutes.

- Remove to a plate with a paper towel while you cook the remaining shrimp. Feel free to place it in the oven at the lowest setting to keep warm.
- Serve with Chipotle Cocktail Sauce!

Nutrition Information

- Calories: 465| Total Fat: 28g| Saturated Fat: 9g| Unsaturated Fat: 17g| Cholesterol: 170mg| Sodium: 2119mg| Carbohydrates: 14g| Fiber: 1g| Sugar: 5g| Protein: 37g

12. Best Air Fryer Fish Recipes

Prep Time: 5 Minutes

Cook Time: 10 Minutes

Total Time: 15 Minutes

Ingredients

- 2 (6 ounces) skin-on salmon fillets, preferably wild-caught
- 2 tablespoons butter, melted
- 2 cloves garlic, minced (about 1 teaspoon)
- 1 teaspoon fresh italian parsley, chopped (or 1/4 teaspoon dried
- Salt and pepper, to taste

Instructions

- Preheat the air fryer to 360 degrees.
- Season the fresh salmon with salt and pepper then mix the melted butter, garlic, and parsley in a bowl.
- Baste the salmon fillets with the garlic butter mixture and carefully place the salmon inside the air fryer side-by-side with the skin side down.
- Cook for approximately 10 minutes until salmon flakes easily with a knife or fork.

- Eat immediately or store in the refrigerator for up to 3 days.

Nutrition Information

- Calories: 341| Total Fat: 26g| Saturated Fat: 10g| Trans Fat: 0g| Unsaturated Fat: 13g| Cholesterol: 102mg| Sodium: 309mg| Carbohydrates: 1g| Fiber: 0g| Sugar: 0g| Protein: 25g

13. Air Fryer Spicy Shrimp Recipe

Prep Time: 10 minutes

Cook Time: 7 minutes

Ingredients

- 1 pound large, raw shrimp tail on
- 1 tsp. avocado oil
- 1 tsp. chili powder
- 1/2 tsp. paprika powder
- 1/4 tsp. garlic powder
- 1/2 tsp. kosher salt
- 1/2 tsp. black pepper
- 1/4 tsp. ground cayenne pepper -or more if desired.

- 1/4 tsp. dried thyme
- 1/4 tsp. dried oregano
- 1/4 tsp. ground cumin
- 1/4 tsp. ground dried mustard

Instructions

- Thaw raw shrimp (if frozen) and place on a paper plate with paper towels and dab dry.
- Preheat the air fryer oven to 400º F for 5 minutes.
- Meanwhile, in a small bowl, combine the spices:
- chili powder, paprika, garlic powder, salt, pepper, cayenne, thyme, oregano, cumin, and ground mustard. Stir to combine.
- Drizzle the thawed shrimp with avocado (or olive) oil and toss the shrimp in this spice mixture.
- Place shrimp in preheated air fryer basket and spread out in a single layer for even cooking. Spray the shrimp with cooking spray if desired. Place in the air fryer and bake for 7 minutes. Flip halfway through if desired but not required.
- This is great to eat alone, on lettuce wraps, burritos, over rice or whatever else sounds good to you! It's healthy and delicious and I hope you enjoy it!

Nutrition Value

- Calories: 106.2kcal | Carbohydrates: 1.1g | Protein: 0.8g | Fat: 11.3g | Saturated Fat: 7g | Cholesterol: 36.4mg | Sodium: 605.4mg | Potassium: 9mg | Fiber: 0.1g | Sugar: 0.1g | Vitamin C: 0.7mg | Calcium: 8.4mg | Iron: 0.1mg

14. Crispy Air Fryer Shrimp

Prep Time: 10 Minutes

Cook Time: 20 Minutes

Total Time: 30 Minutes

Ingredients

- ¼ Cup flour
- 1 ½ teaspoon lemon pepper seasoning
- ½ teaspoon garlic powder
- ½ teaspoon salt or to taste
- ⅓ cup seasoned bread crumbs

- ⅓ cup panko bread crumbs
- 2 large eggs beaten
- ¾ pound large shrimp with tails peeled and deveined
- Cooking spray

Instructions

- Combine flour and half of the seasonings. In a separate bowl, combine bread crumbs and remaining seasonings.
- Preheat the air fryer to 400°F for 5 minutes.
- Toss shrimp in the flour mixture. Remove a shrimp from the flour mixture and dip in egg and then into the breadcrumb mixture. Repeat with remaining shrimp.
- Lightly spray shrimp with cooking spray.
- Add a single layer of shrimp to the air fryer basket. Cook 4 minutes.
- Flip shrimp over, spritz with cooking spray, and cook an additional 4 minutes or just until cooked through and crispy.
- Repeat with remaining shrimp.
- Serve with cocktail sauce.

Nutrition Information

- Calories: 210| Carbohydrates: 17g| Protein: 24g| Fat: 4g| Saturated Fat: 1g| Cholesterol: 307mg|

15. Southwest Air Fryer Shrimp

Prep Time: 4 Minutes

Cook Time: 6 Minutes

Total Time: 10 Minutes

Ingredients

- 1 lb. peeled, deveined shrimp (large or extra-large, such as 26-30 size)
- 1 teaspoon extra-virgin olive oil
- 1 1/2 teaspoons southwestern seasoning (see notes)

Instructions

- Preheat the Air Fryer to 400 (if yours requires preheating).
- Pat the peeled and deveined shrimp dry with a paper towel and place in a bowl or on a plate.
- Drizzle the shrimp with olive oil and sprinkle with the southwestern seasoning mix. Toss the shrimp to get them all well coated.
- Place the shrimp in the tray of the Air Fryer. Cook at 400 for 6-8 minutes, until the shrimp are cooked through.
- Serve and enjoy!

Nutrition Information

- Calories: 146| total Fat: 3g| saturated Fat: 1g| trans Fat: 0g| unsaturated Fat: 2g| cholesterol: 239mg| sodium: 1644mg| carbohydrates: 2g| fiber: 0g| sugar: 0g| protein: 26g

16. Air Fryer Salmon

Prep time: 10 minutes

Cook time: 7 minutes

Total time: 17 mins

Ingredients

- 2 salmon fillets (about 1 1/2-inches thick)
- 2 teaspoons olive oil

Dry Rub:

- 2 teaspoons smoked paprika

- 1 tablespoon brown sugar (optional)
- 1 tablespoon garlic powder
- 1 teaspoon onion powder
- 1/2 teaspoon ginger powder
- 1/4 teaspoon red pepper flakes
- 1/2 teaspoon salt
- 1/4 teaspoon ground black pepper

Instructions

- Remove fish from the fridge, inspect it for any bones, and let it sit on the counter for an hour.
- Mix the RUB ingredients in a bowl.
- Rub each fillet with olive oil and after that the dry rub mixture.
- Place fillets in the basket of the air fryer.
- Set air fryer at 390 degrees for 7 minutes if the filets are 1-1/2-inches thick.
- When the timer goes off, check fillets with a fork to make sure they are done to your desired doneness. If needed cook a few minutes longer. Cooking time will vary based on the temperature of the fish and the size. It is better to set the air fryer for a little less time and add a few more minutes if needed, to avoid overcooking the fish.

Nutrition Information

- Calories: 325| Carbohydrates: 11g| Protein: 35g| Fat: 15g| Saturated Fat: 2g| Cholesterol: 94g| Sodium: 667mg| Potassium: 926g| Fiber: 1g Sugar: 6g| Calcium: 20| Iron: 2g

17. Air-Fried Coconut Shrimp

Active Time: 15 Mins

Total Time: 30 Mins

Ingredients

- 1/2 cup (about 2 1/8 oz.) all-purpose flour 1 1/2 teaspoons black pepper 2 large eggs 2/3 cup unsweetened flaked coconut 1/3 cup panko (Japanese-style breadcrumbs) 12 ounces medium peeled, deveined raw shrimp, tail-on (about 24 shrimp) Cooking spray 1/2 teaspoon kosher salt 1/4 cup honey 1/4 cup lime juice 1 serrano chile, thinly sliced 2 teaspoons chopped fresh cilantro (optional)

How To Make It

- Stir together flour and pepper in a shallow dish. Lightly beat eggs in a second shallow dish. Stir together coconut and panko in a third shallow dish. Holding each shrimp by the tail, dredge shrimp in flour mixture, making sure not to coat tail; shake off excess. Dip in egg, allowing any excess to drip off. Dredge in coconut mixture, pressing to adhere. Coat shrimp well with cooking spray.

- Place half of the shrimp in the air fryer basket, and cook at 400°F until golden, 6 to 8 minutes, turning shrimp over halfway through cooking. Season with 1/4 teaspoon of the salt. Repeat with remaining shrimp and salt.

- While shrimp cook, whisk together honey, lime juice, and serrano chile in a small bowl. Sprinkle shrimp with cilantro, if desired. Serve with sauce.

Nutritional Information

- Calories: 250| Fat: 9g| Sat fat: 7g| Un sat fat: 1g| Protein: 15g| Carbohydrate: 30g| Fiber: 2g |Sugars: 18 |Added sugars: 17g |Sodium: 527mg

18. Air Fryer Scallops

Prep Time: 5 Minutes

Cook Time: 10 Minutes

Total Time: 15 Minutes

Ingredients

- 6 fresh scallops
- ½ teaspoon salt
- ¼ teaspoon pepper
- 3 Tablespoons butter
- 1 garlic clove, minced

- 1 teaspoon lemon juice
- 1 teaspoon chopped fresh chives

Instructions

- Rinse scallops and dry thoroughly.
- Season the scallops with salt and pepper on both sides.
- Prepare the air fryer basket with cooking spray and place the scallops in the basket, evenly apart.
- Cook at 400 degrees for 10 minutes, flipping them over halfway through cooking.
- While the scallops are cooking, add garlic to the butter and melt in the microwave or stovetop. Add the lemon juice and chives and stir together.
- When the scallops are done cooking, place them on a plate and drizzle the lemon garlic butter over them. Serve immediately.

Nutrition Value

- Calories: 199| Total Fat: 18g| Saturated Fat: 11g| Trans Fat: 1g| UnsaturatedFat:5g| Cholesterol: 62mg| Sodium: 927mg| Carbohydrates: 3g| Sugar: 0g| Protein: 8g

19. Air fryer shrimp

Prep Time: 3 minutes

Cook Time: 10 minutes

Ingredients

- 1 lb large raw shrimp peeled, deveined, tail on
- 1 garlic clove pressed
- 1/4 tsp Salt
- Pinch of pepper
- 1/2 tsp Cajun seasoning
- 1 Tbsp olive oil

Instructions

- Take your peeled and deveined shrimp and pat them dry with a paper towel.
- Now place the shrimp in a large bowl along with the pressed garlic, salt, pepper, Cajun seasoning, and olive oil.
- Toss everything together using tongs. From here you can cover it with plastic wrap and let the shrimp marinate in the refrigerator for about one hour or you can cook them right away.
- To cook the shrimp in the air fryer, set your basket air fryer on the shrimp setting or set the temperature to

350 degrees Fahrenheit and cook for 8-10 minutes flipping them halfway through.

Nutrition

- Calories: 146kcal | Carbohydrates: 1g | Protein: 23g | Fat: 5g | Saturated Fat: 1g | Cholesterol: 286mg | Sodium: 1027mg | Potassium: 91mg | Fiber: 1g | Sugar: 1g | Vitamin C: 5mg | Calcium: 164mg | Iron: 2mg

20. Air Fryer Spring Shrimp

Prep Time: 5 Minutes

Cook Time: 5 Minutes

Total Time: 10 Minutes

Ingredients

- 1 pound medium shrimp (36/40 shrimp)
- 1 Tablespoon olive oil
- 2 teaspoons paprika *see notes for other seasoning ideas
- 1 teaspoon onion powder

- 1 teaspoon garlic powder
- 1/2 teaspoon salt
- 1/2 teaspoon pepper

Instructions

- Preheat the air fryer to 400 F for 5 minutes. Don't skip the preheating for this recipe!
- Peel and devein the shrimp if necessary. You can either leave the tails on or take them off, whichever you prefer.
- In a small bowl combine the paprika, onion powder, garlic powder, salt, and pepper.
- Add the shrimp to a large bowl and drizzle with olive oil. Then sprinkle the seasonings over the shrimp and toss everything so the shrimp is coated in seasoning.
- Add the shrimp to the preheated air fryer basket. Keep the shrimp in a single layer. Depending on the size of your air fryer basket you might need to make two batches.
- Cook at 400 F for 5 minutes, flipping the shrimp with a spatula halfway through.
- Serve with parsley, lemons, and melted butter, or add them to a salad or tacos.

Nutrition Value

- Calories: 173| Total Fat: 5g| Saturated Fat: 1g| Trans Fat: 0g| Unsaturated Fat: 4g| Cholesterol: 239mg| Sodium: 1340mg| Carbohydrates: 4g| Fiber: 1g| Sugar: 0g| Protein: 26g

21. Air Fryer Bang Bang Shrimp

Prep Time: 5 Minutes

Cook Time: 5 Minutes

Total Time: 10 Minutes

Ingredients

- 1 Pound uncooked shrimp deveined
- Buttermilk
- 1/2 cup cornstarch
- Olive oil for spraying
- Bang Bang Sauce
- 1/2 cup mayonnaise
- 1/4 cup sweet chili sauce
- 2 tsp sriracha sauce

Instructions

- Preheat Air fryer to 375
- Dip Shrimp in buttermilk
- Shake off excess liquid
- Coat each one in cornstarch
- Spray each one with olive oil
- Place in the air fryer for 4 minutes turn over and cook for an additional one minute or until golden brown
- Meanwhile mix mayo, sweet chili sauce, and sriracha sauce.

- When shrimp are done toss them in the bang bang sauce.

Nutrition Value

- Calories: 168| total Fat: 10g| saturated Fat: 2g| trans Fat: 0g| unsaturated Fat: 8g| cholesterol: 63mg| sodium: 403mg| carbohydrates: 11g| fiber: 0g| sugar: 5g| protein: 7g

22. Air Fryer Scallops

Prep Time: 15 minutes

Cook Time: 10 minutes

Ingredients

- 12 oz frozen scallops thawed and patted dry
- 16 slices about 2 oz precooked center cut bacon
- 1 tablespoon olive oil
- 2 teaspoons seafood or cajun seasoning

Instructions

- Wrap one piece of bacon around the edges of scallops securing it with a toothpick
- Brush both sides with oil and sprinkle with seasoning
- Place in air fryer basket in a single layer
- Cook at 400 degrees for 4 minutes, flip and continue cooking until cooked through until tender and opaque (about another 4 minutes)

Nutrition Value

- Calories: 195kcal | Carbohydrates: 3g | Protein: 17g | Fat: 12g | Saturated Fat: 4g | Cholesterol: 41mg | Sodium: 707mg | Potassium: 287mg | Fiber: 1g | Sugar: 1g | Calcium: 7mg | Iron: 1mg

23. Air Fryer Popcorn Shrimp

Prep Time: 20 Minutes

Cook Time: 5 Minutes

Ingredients

- 20-24 frozen medium shrimp, peeled, deveined, tails on (I like using 31-40)
- 1 large egg, beaten
- ⅓ cup cornmeal

- ½ tsp. Salt
- Oil spray

Instructions

- Place frozen shrimp in a large colander and run cold water over them until thawed for about 10 minutes. Transfer to a paper towel-lined plate and pat dry.
- In a small bowl good for dipping beat the egg. And in another small bowl mix the cornmeal and salt (you can even through in some spices here!).
- Heat the air fryer to 360°F.
- Working one at a time, dip each shrimp into the egg batter and then into the cornmeal making sure the cornmeal creates an even coat. Place on a wire rack.
- Once heated, remove the basket from the air fryer, spray with oil and place the shrimp in the basket creating an even layer. Spray again with oil and cook for 2 to 3 minutes on each side. Serve with your favorite sauce!

Nutritional Value

- Calories: 460| Protein 28.9g| Carbohydrates 40.2g| Dietary Fiber 9.9g| Sugars 4.5g| Fat 22.1g| Saturated Fat 3.2g| Calcium 113.2mg|

24. Air-Fried Salt And Pepper Shrimp

Prep Time: 20 Mins

Cook Time: 30 Mins

Total Time: 50 Mins

Ingredients

- 1 cup all-purpose flour
- ½ cup cornstarch
- 2 teaspoons salt
- 2 teaspoons coarsely ground black pepper

- 1 pound extra-large shrimp peeled and deveined with tails left on
- 2 eggs
- Canola or vegetable oil
- 1 teaspoon olive oil
- 2 cloves garlic thinly sliced
- 1-inch ginger thinly sliced
- 4 cherry peppers sliced
- 3 scallions chopped

Instructions

- Set up a dredging station. Combine the flour, cornstarch, salt, and black pepper and divide the mixture between two zipper sealable plastic bags. Beat the eggs together in a bowl. Add the shrimp to one bag of flour and shake them around to coat. Working in batches, remove the shrimp from the bag of flour, shaking off any excess, and dip each shrimp in the beaten eggs before placing them in the second bag of flour and shaking to coat again. Set the coated shrimp aside.
- Pre-heat air fryer to 400°F.
- Transfer the coated shrimp to the air fryer basket and spritz generously with oil.

- Air-fry the shrimp in batches for 6 minutes. Flip the shrimp over, spritz with oil again and air-fry for an additional 2 minutes.
- While the shrimp is cooking, heat the olive oil in a sauté pan. Add the garlic, ginger, and cherry peppers and sauté for three minutes, until the peppers have softened slightly.
- When the last batch of shrimp has finished cooking. Load all the shrimp back into the air fryer and air-fry at 370°F 1 to 2 minutes, until all the shrimp is heated through.
- Toss with cherry peppers and scallions before serving.

Nutrition Facts

- Calories: 286| Protein 24g| Carbohydrates 30.4g| Dietary Fiber 6.9g| Sugars 3.5g| Fat 9.3g| Calcium 117.8mg| Iron 1.6mg| Magnesium 87.2mg| Potassium 662.1mg| Sodium 442.7mg.

25. Air Fryer Coconut Shrimp

Prep Time: 15 Min

Cook Time: 25 Min

Total Time: 40 Min

Ingredients

- ½ cup flour
- 2 tsp. salt
- 1 tsp. pepper
- 2 eggs, beaten
- ½ cup panko breadcrumbs

- 1 cup unsweetened shredded coconut
- 12 oz deveined, tail-off raw shrimp

Dipping Sauce

- ¼ cup red pepper jelly
- 2 tsp. bottled ginger
- 2 tsp. apple cider vinegar
- 2 tsp. minced garlic
- ¼ cup lightly packed fresh mint
- ¼ tsp. salt
- ⅛ tsp. pepper

Directions

- In a shallow dish, add the flour and season with salt and pepper.
- In a separate shallow dish, add the beaten eggs. In a final shallow dish combine the breadcrumbs and coconut.
- Working in batches, toss 1/3 of the shrimp in the flour, then the egg, and finally in the coconut mixture. Coat both sides of the shrimp well in coconut mixture. Place on a large cutting board and repeat with the remaining shrimp.
- Place baking rack in the bowl in the high position and place 12 shrimp on top.

- Tap the grill button and set the temperature to 400°F and fry for 6-7 minutes. Repeat with remaining shrimp.
- Meanwhile, in the bowl of a small food processor, add all of the sauce ingredients and mix on low speed until mint is finely chopped.
- Serve hot coconut shrimp with dipping sauce.

Nutrition Facts

- Calories: 334| Protein 31g| Carbohydrates 25.7g| Dietary Fiber 2.1g| Sugars 4.2g| Fat 10.2g| Saturated Fat 1.5g| Calcium 97.2mg| Iron 5.3mg| Magnesium 77.1mg| Potassium 902.6mg| Sodium 770.3mg.

26. Air Fryer Coconut Shrimp With Dipping Sauce

Prep Time: 10 minutes

Cook Time: 9 minutes

Total Time: 19 minutes

Ingredients

- 1 lb large raw shrimp peeled and deveined with tail on
- 2 eggs beaten
- ½ cup All-Purpose Flour
- ½ cup unsweetened shredded coconut
- ¼ cup Panko Breadcrumbs
- 1 tsp salt
- ¼ tsp black pepper
- Oil for spraying

Instructions

- Clean and dry shrimp. Set aside.
- Grab 3 bowls. Place flour in one bowl. Place beaten egg in the second bowl. Combine coconut, breadcrumbs, salt, and black pepper in the third bowl.
- Preheat your Air Fryer to 390 degrees Fahrenheit. This should take about 3 minutes.

- Dip each shrimp in flour, then egg, then coconut mixture, ensuring shrimp is covered on all sides during each dip.
- Place shrimp in a single layer in an air fryer basket that has been greased.
- Lightly spray the shrimp with oil and then close the Air Fryer basket. Cook for 4 minutes.
- After 4 minutes, open-air fryer basket and flip shrimp over. Spray shrimp again, close the air fryer basket and cook for 5 more minutes.
- Remove shrimp from the basket and serve with Thai Sweet Chili Sauce. Enjoy

Nutritional Value

- Calories:293kcal|Carbohydrates:17g | Protein: 28g | Fat: 11g | Saturated Fat: 7g | Cholesterol: 367mg | Sodium: 1525mg | Potassium: 200mg | Fiber: 2g | Sugar: 1g | Vitamin C: 4.6mg | Calcium: 187mg | Iron: 4.1mg

27. Air Fryer Fish Recipe (Crispy Air Fryer Tilapia)

Prep Time: 10 minutes

Cook Time: 15 minutes

Total Time: 25 minutes

Ingredients

- 4 Tilapia Fish Fillet, you may use any light fish fillet
- 2 Cups Bread Crumbs, you can use homemade or storebought
- 1 Large Egg

- 1 Tsp Warm Water, to whisk eggs
- Olive Oil Spray, for cooking the fish
- Aluminum Foil, to add as a liner in the air-fryer basket

Seasoning:

- 2 Tbsp Lemon Pepper Seasoning
- 2 Tbsp Paprika Powder, you can use other chili powder too
- 1 Tsp Dry Garlic Powder
- 1 Tbsp Salt, use as per taste

Instructions

Prep-Work:

- In a large bowl, whisk together the egg with 1 tsp warm water. Keep aside.
- In another large bowl, add bread crumbs, seasoning ingredients, and whisk to mix everything. Keep aside.
- Take the aluminum foil and place it into the air-fryer basket as a liner.
- Make the Air Fryer Fish Recipe
- Now take each fish fillet and dip it into the whisked egg bowl. Coat both sides of the fish evenly.
- Drip any excess egg in the egg bowl.
- Place the egg coated fish in the bread crumbs bowl. Coat both the side evenly.

- Tap off any excess bread crumbs and place the coated fish fillet on a clean plate.
- Similarly, coat all the fish fillet and keep aside.
- Take the air-fryer basket and place 1-2 fish fillet (mine could only accommodate 1 fillet).
- Spray with olive oil and turn On the Air-Fryer at 350f for 10 minutes.
- After 10 minutes, turn the fish upside down and air-fry again for 5 minutes to brown the other side.
- Once the fish is golden brown on both sides, remove and place on a clean plate.
- Similarly, air-fry all the remaining fish fillet.
- Once everything is cooked, serve the fish fillet with Cucumber Avocado Salad.

Nutrition Information

- Calories: 350| Total Fat: 15g| Saturated Fat: 4g| Trans Fat: 0g| Unsaturated Fat: 10g| Cholesterol: 130mg| Sodium: 400mg| Carbohydrates: 43g| Fiber: 5g| Sugar: 4g| Protein: 76g

28. Easy Air Fryer Breaded Sea Scallops

Prep Time: 15 Minutes

Cook Time: 15 Minutes

Total Time: 30 Minutes

Ingredients

- 12 oz fresh sea scallops, defrosted
- 2 tbsp olive oil
- 1/2 tsp sea salt
- 1/2 tsp ground black pepper
- 1/2 tsp garlic powder
- 1/2 tsp onion powder
- 1/4 cup traditional bread crumbs
- 1 tsp Old Bay seasoning

Instructions

- Add olive oil to a large bowl, or resealable bag. Add scallops and coat thoroughly.
- Combine the salt, pepper, garlic, and onion powder into a second bowl, or bag. Transfer scallops from olive oil to seasonings and tosses to coat.
- Combine bread crumbs and Old Bay seasoning to third bowl, or bag. Transfer scallops from seasonings to bread crumb mixture and tosses to coat.

- Remove the basket from the air fryer and lightly spray with nonstick cooking spray. Space out the scallops in the basket. You may need to cook scallops in a couple of batches so they aren't overcrowded.
- Cook at 400° for 12 minutes. Up to 15 minutes if the scallops are larger, reaching an internal temperature of 145°.

Nutrition Information

- Calories: 189| total Fat: 10g| saturated Fat: 1g| trans Fat: 0g| unsaturated Fat: 8g| cholesterol: 12mg| sodium: 725mg| carbohydrates: 10g| fiber: 1g| sugar: 1g| protein: 15g

29. Air Fryer Cajun Shrimp

Prep Time 5 minutes

Cook Time 6 minutes

Total Time 11 minutes

Ingredients

- 1/2 lb shrimp peeled and deveined
- 3/4 tsp cayenne pepper
- 1/2 tsp old bay seasoning
- 1/4 tsp smoked paprika
- 1 tbsp olive oil

- 1 pinch salt

Instructions

- Press "Pre-Heat," set temperature at 390F, and set the cooking time at 6 minutes. Press "Start."
- Add all ingredients to the mixing bowl and mix until shrimp is completely coated.
- Place shrimp in Fry Pan Basket and cook.

Nutritional Value

- Calories: 217| Protein 25.9g| Carbohydrates 15.7g| Fat 7g| Cholesterol 50.4mg| Sodium 198.3mg.

30. Air Fryer Shrimp Boil Recipe

Prep Time: 15 Minutes

Cook Time: 15 Minutes

Total Time: 30 Minutes

Ingredients

- 1 pound baby yellow potatoes sliced
- 3 ears corn, cut crosswise into 3 to 6 pieces
- 1/2 cup unsalted butter, melted
- 6 cloves garlic, minced
- 2 tablespoon Old Bay seasoning
- 1 pound medium shrimp, peeled and deveined
- 1 (12.8-ounce) package smoked andouille sausage, sliced
- 2 tablespoons chopped fresh parsley leaves
- 1 lemon, cut into wedges (optional)

Instructions

- Preheat air fryer or air fryer oven to 400 degrees F.
- Lightly coat your airflow tray or fryer basket with nonstick spray.
- In a large pot or Instant Pot (about 4 mins high pressure) with salted water parboil potatoes and corn, just until tender.

- In a large bowl, combine butter, garlic, and Old Bay seasoning.
- Stir everything together with the butter mixture, combine well.
- Place into the air fryer or air fryer oven and bake for 6-8 minutes, or until the shrimp is pink
- Serve immediately with optional lemon wedges, garnished with parsley, if desired.

Nutrition Information

- Calories: 392
- Total Fat: 21g
- Saturated Fat: 11g
- Trans Fat: 0g
- Unsaturated Fat: 8g
- Cholesterol: 207mg
- Sodium: 1565mg
- Carbohydrates: 31g
- Fiber: 4g
- Sugar: 4g
- Protein: 23g

31. Fish Cakes

Cook Time: 11Mins

Ingredients

- 1-4 Single Serve   Fish Cakes

Method

- Preheat the air fryer to 180 ° C or 360 ° F. This is usually around 3 minutes.
- Place the frozen fish cakes into the basket of the air fryer.
- Cook for 11 minutes

Nutritional Value

- Calories: 107

32. Hoisin Glazed Air Fryer Salmon

Prep Time: 5 Minutes

Cook Time: 10 Minutes

Total Time: 15 Minutes

Ingredients

- 2 5 ounce salmon fillets, skin on
- Pinch of kosher salt
- Pinch of black pepper
- 1 tablespoon hoisin sauce
- 1 teaspoon low-sodium soy sauce
- 1 teaspoon light brown sugar
- 1 clove garlic, minced (1/2 teaspoon minced garlic)
- 1/2 teaspoon minced fresh ginger
- 1/2 teaspoon rice wine (or white) vinegar
- 1/2 teaspoon sesame seeds, optional
- 1/2 teaspoon finely chopped fresh parsley, optional

Instructions

- If your air fryer requires preheating, do so now at 400 degrees F for 5 minutes.
- Season the salmon fillets with kosher salt and pepper to taste.

- In a small bowl, whisk together the hoisin, soy sauce, brown sugar, garlic, ginger, and vinegar. Brush the glaze all over the salmon.
- Spray the basket grates of the air fryer with cooking spray.
- Place the salmon fillets skin side down onto the basket grates, making sure they're not touching.
- Air fry for 10 minutes or until an internal temperature reaches at least 145 degrees F.
- Sprinkle with the sesame seeds and parsley. Serve right away and enjoy!

Nutrition Value

- Calories:274kcal | Carbohydrates: 6g | Protein: 34g | Fat: 11g | Saturated Fat: 2g | Cholesterol: 94mg | Sodium: 288mg | Potassium: 833mg | Fiber: 1g | Sugar: 4g | Vitamin C: 1mg | Calcium: 20mg | Iron: 1mg

33. Keto Air Fryer Fish Sticks

Prep Time: 10 Minutes

Cook Time: 15 Minutes

Total Time: 25 Minutes

Ingredients

- 12 oz tilapia loins, cut into fish sticks
- 4 tablespoons of mayonnaise
- 1 teaspoon of garlic powder
- 1 teaspoon of paprika
- 3.25 oz bag of pork rinds crushed into crumbs

- 1/2 cup grated parmesan cheese

Instructions

- Thaw the tilapia loins if they are frozen. Dab dry with a paper towel.
- Cut the fish into fish stick sized pieces. This will depend on the size and shape of your tilapia loins but use your judgment. I had 3 pieces and got about 20 pieces.
- In a food processor, add the pork rinds and crush them to make crumbs. Add the parmesan cheese and spices and pulse to mix through. Then pour into a shallow bowl.
- Add the fish to a ziplock bag with the mayo. Squish the bag to try to get the mayo all over the fish pieces.
- Take out the fish, 1 piece at a time, and roll in the pork rind mixture.
- Place the coated fish sticks into the air fryer. Spray the air fryer basket first.
- Set the temperature to 380°F and cook for 15 minutes until brown and crunchy.

Nutrition Information

- Calories: 75| Net Carbohydrates: 0.1g

34. Crispy Golden Air Fryer Fish

Prep Time: 2 Mins

Cook Time: 14 Mins

Total Time: 19 Mins

Ingredients

- 2 tbsp cornmeal polenta
- 2 tsp cajun seasoning
- ½ tsp paprika
- ½ tsp garlic powder
- Sea salt flakes to taste
- 2 catfish fillets

- Low-calorie spray

Instructions

- Preheat air fryer to 400F (200C).
- Mix the first 5 ingredients and then add to a Ziploc bag.
- Rinse the catfish, pat dry, and add fillets to the Ziploc bag.
- Seal the bag and then shake until the fillets are fully coated.
- Place the coated fillets in the air fryer basket. (if you have a small fryer you will need to cook them one at a time).
- Spray the fillets with low-calorie spray, close the air fryer and cook for 10 mins.
- Turn the air fried fish fillets over and cook for an additional 3-4 mins, or until done.

Nutrition Value

- Calories: 212kcal | Carbohydrates: 9g | Protein: 35g | Fat: 3g | Saturated Fat: 1g | Cholesterol: 85mg | Sodium: 91mg | Potassium: 598mg | Fiber: 1g | Calcium: 22mg | Iron: 1.9mg

35. Fish En Papillote | Air Fryer Fish In Parchment Paper

Prep Time: 10 minutes

Cook Time: 15 minutes

Total Time: 25 minutes

Ingredients

- 2 5-oz (2) Cod Fillets, thawed
- 1/2 cup (64 g) julienned carrots
- 1/2 cup (43.5 g) julienned fennel bulbs, or 1/4 cup julienned celery
- 1/2 cup (74.5 g) thinly sliced red peppers
- 2 (2) sprigs tarragon, or 1/2 teaspoon dried tarragon
- 2 pats (2 pats) melted butter
- 1 tablespoon (1 tablespoon) Lemon Juice

- 1 tablespoon (1 tablespoon) Kosher Salt, divided
- 1/2 teaspoon (0.5 teaspoons) Ground Black Pepper
- 1 tablespoon (1 tablespoon) Oil

Instructions

- In a medium bowl combine melted butter, tarragon, 1/2 teaspoon salt, and lemon juice. Mix well until you get a creamy sauce. Add the julienned vegetable and mix well. Set aside.
- Cut two squares of parchment large enough o hold the fish and vegetables.
- Spray the fish fillets with oil and apply salt and pepper to both sides of the fillets.
- Lay one filet down on each parchment square. Top each fillet with half the vegetables. Pour any remaining sauce over the vegetables.
- Fold over the parchment paper and crimp the sides to hold fish, veggies, and sauce securely inside the packet. Place the packets inside the air fryer basket.
- Set your air fryer to 350F for 15 minutes. Remove each packet to a plate and open it just before serving.

Nutrition Value

- Calories: 251kcal | Carbohydrates: 8g | Protein: 26g | Fat: 12g | Fiber: 2g | Sugar: 3g

36. Air Fryer Shrimp Tacos

Prep Time: 10 Mins

Cook Time: 25 Mins

Total Time: 35 Mins

Ingredients

- 2 tsp. Garlic powder
- 2 tsp. Onion powder
- 1 tsp. Cumin
- 1 tsp. Chili powder
- ½ tsp. Kosher salt
- ½ tsp. Pepper
- ¾ cup gluten-free flour blend or ap flour if not gluten-free
- 3 eggs
- 1 cup gluten-free panko breadcrumbs or regular panko breadcrumbs if not gluten-free
- 1 lb. Shrimp
- Cooking oil spray

For The Sauce:

- ½ Cup sour cream
- ¼ cup mayo
- 1 large lemon zest and juice
- ½ tsp. Garlic powder

- Pinch salt and pepper
- 1 package corn tortillas
- Toppings of choice such as tomatoes, avocado, lettuce optional

Instructions

- Thaw and remove tails from 1 lb. of shrimp.
- Place the thawed shrimp between two rows of paper towels and pat dry.
- Place ¾ cup of a gluten-free flour blend – I love Bob's Red Mill 1 to 1 Flour (or regular AP flour if not gluten-free) in a small bowl.
- In another bowl crack 3 eggs and whisk with a small whisk or a fork.
- Add 1 cup of Gluten-Free Panko Breadcrumbs (or regular Panko breadcrumbs if not GF) to a third bowl along with 2 tsp. each of garlic powder and onion powder, 1 tsp. each of cumin and chili powder, and ½ tsp. kosher salt and pepper. Stir until completely combined.
- Dip the shrimp (one at a time) first in the flour making sure it is entirely coated. Next, dip the shrimp in the eggs. Third, dip the shrimp in the Panko breadcrumb mixture making sure it is entirely coated. Repeat with the remainder of the shrimp.

- Place the breaded shrimp on a plate and mist or baste both sides with cooking oil. (They should be coated but not saturated in oil).
- Place as many shrimp as will fit in the basket without overcrowding it. Once the basket is in the Air Fryer set the temperature to 370 degrees and cook for 4 minutes on the first side. Flip the shrimp over and cook for another 4 minutes on the second side.
- Remove the shrimp from the basket, set aside, and repeat this process until all the shrimp have cooked.

For The Sauce:

- Add ½ cup sour cream and ¼ cup mayo to a small bowl. Grate the zest of 1 lemon into the bowl using a Microplane or small zester. Cut the lemon and half and add the juice of the entire lemon. Add ½ tsp. garlic powder and a generous pinch of salt and pepper.
- Stir until completely combined using a small whisk or fork.
- To Serve: Serve shrimp on warmed tortillas with a generous amount of sauce. Garnish with your favorite toppings such as cabbage, tomatoes, lettuce, spinach, avocado, guacamole, pico de gallo, pickled onions or radishes, or hot sauce (optional).

Nutrition Value

- Calories: 464kcal
- Carbohydrates: 53g
- Protein: 24g
- Fat: 18g
- Saturated Fat: 5g
- Cholesterol: 295mg
- Sodium: 992mg
- Potassium: 274mg
- Fiber: 6g
- Sugar: 2g
- Vitamin A: 492IU
- Vitamin C: 13mg
- Calcium: 204mg
- Iron: 4mg

37. Air Fryer Cajun Shrimp

Prep Time: 2 mins

Cook Time: 6 mins

Total Time: 8 mins

Ingredients

- 30 Frozen Shrimp
- ½ Tsp Extra Virgin Olive Oil
- 1 Tbsp Cajun Seasoning
- 1 Tsp Garlic Puree
- Salt & Pepper
- 1 Lime juice only
- 1 Tsp Cajun Seasoning optional

Instructions

- Count out and remove 30 frozen shrimp from your freezer bag.
- Load into a mixing bowl with your cajun seasoning, extra virgin olive oil, salt, pepper, and garlic.
- Toss and load into the air fryer basket.
- Cook for 6 minutes at 180c/360f.
- Once cooked sprinkle with extra cajun seasoning and the juice of a lime.

Nutrition Value

- Calories: 125kcal | Carbohydrates: 7g | Protein: 19g | Fat: 3g | Saturated Fat: 1g | Cholesterol: 227mg | Sodium: 703mg | Potassium: 209mg | Fiber: 3g | Sugar: 1g | Vitamin C: 14mg | Calcium: 150mg | Iron: 3mg

38. Spicy Shrimp Patties Recipe (Air Fryer Shrimp)

Prep Time: 15 mins

Cook Time: 25 mins

Ingredients

- 1 lb wild-caught shrimp peeled & deveined
- 1 tablespoon avocado oil or any oil of your choice
- 1/2 cup red bell pepper finely chopped
- 1 clove garlic finely chopped
- 1/4 cup red onion finely chopped

- 1/4 cup cilantro finely chopped
- 1/4 cup green onion finely chopped
- 1/2 small jalapeno seeded & finely chopped
- 1 1/2 cup panko breadcrumbs divided
- 1 egg
- 3 tablespoons mayo
- 1 1/2 teaspoon hot pepper sauce or to taste
- 1 tablespoon lime juice freshly squeezed
- 1/2 teaspoon organic sugar
- Salt & pepper to taste

Instructions

- Using a food processor, add 1 lb shrimp & pulse until tiny pieces, transfer chopped shrimp to a mixing bowl. Set aside.
- Preheat 1 tablespoon of oil in a skillet, then add 1/2 cup chopped bell pepper and saute for 3 minutes. Next, add 1 clove of chopped garlic and saute for 1 minute, stirring few times. Turn off the heat.
- While bell pepper is cooling, preheat the Air Fryer to 400F. Combine the rest of the ingredients into the shrimp bowl: 1/4 cup of red onion, 1/4 cup of cilantro, 1/4 cup green onion, 1/2 of small jalapeno, 1/2 cup Panko breadcrumbs, 1 egg, 3 tablespoons of mayo, 1 1/2 teaspoon of hot pepper sauce, 1 tablespoon of lime

juice, 1/2 teaspoon sugar, salt & pepper to taste. Plus saute bell peppers with garlic.

- Give it a good mix. Using hands, form mixture into 12 shrimp patties, coat them in 1 cup of breadcrumbs. Grease the Air Fryer pan with avocado oil and add shrimp patties (try not to crowd them!). Cook for 10 minutes, flipping shrimp patties once on the other side.
- Serve shrimp patties with lime wedges & Avocado Corn Salsa. Enjoy!

Nutrition Value

- Calories: 74kcal | Carbohydrates: 7g | Protein: 2g | Fat: 5g | Saturated Fat: 1g | Cholesterol: 15mg | Sodium: 96mg | Potassium: 43mg | Fiber: 1g | Sugar: 1g | Vitamin C: 10mg | Calcium: 17mg | Iron: 1mg

39. Crab Cakes with Spicy Aioli + Lemon Vinaigrette

Prep Time: 10 minutes

Cook Time: 20 minutes

Total Time: 30 minutes

Ingredients

For The Crab Cakes

- 16 ounces lump crab meat
- 2 tablespoons finely chopped red or orange pepper
- 2 tablespoons finely chopped green onion
- 2 tablespoons olive oil mayonnaise
- 1 tablespoon dijon mustard
- ¼ cup panko breadcrumbs
- ¼ teaspoon ground pepper
- 1 egg, lightly beaten
- Avocado oil spray

For The Aioli

- ¼ cup olive oil mayonnaise
- 1 teaspoon minced shallots
- 1 teaspoon white wine vinegar
- 1 teaspoon dijon mustard
- ¼ teaspoon cayenne pepper

For The Vinaigrette

- 1 tablespoon white wine vinegar
- 1 teaspoon honey
- 4 tablespoons fresh lemon juice, about 1 ½ lemon
- 1 teaspoon lemon zest
- 2 tablespoons extra virgin olive oil

To serve

- 2 cups of baby arugula
- Balsamic glaze, to taste

Instructions

- Make the crab cakes. Combine the crab meat, red pepper, onion, mayonnaise, dijon, panko, and ground pepper in a large bowl. Mix well. Add the egg and mix again until combined. Using about a ¼ cup of the crab mixture form into cakes that are about 1″ thick. Lightly spray them with avocado oil.
- Cook the crab cakes. Arrange the crab cakes in a single layer in your air fryer.
- You'll likely need to cook them in 2-3 batches depending on your air fryer. Cook at 375°F for 10 minutes. Remove from air fryer and keep warm. Repeat if necessary.
- Make the aioli. Mix the mayo, shallots, vinegar, dijon, and cayenne pepper. Set aside until ready to serve.

- Make the vinaigrette. Mix the white wine vinegar, honey, lemon juice, and lemon zest in a small jar. Add the olive oil and mix again until combined.
- Serve. Divide the arugula between two plates. Top with crab cakes. Drizzle with aioli and vinaigrette. If desired add a small drizzle of balsamic glaze.

40. Air Fryer Cajun Salmon Foil Packets

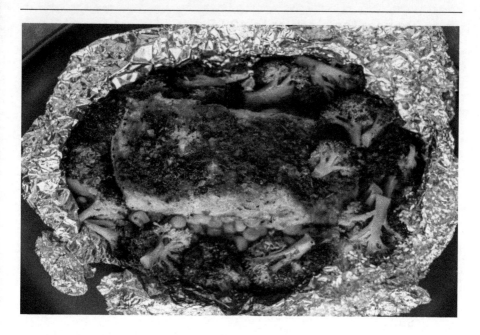

Prep Time: 5 mins

Cook Time: 20 mins

Total Time: 25 mins

Ingredients

- 1 cup canned corn divided
- 2 six oz fresh salmon filets
- 2 cups chopped broccoli divided
- 4 teaspoons Cajun seasoning divided
- 1 tablespoon unsalted butter divided
- Kosher salt to taste
- Lime wedges optional

Instructions

- Preheat the air fryer to 400 F.
- Tear off 2 sheets of aluminum foil about 16-18 inches long and place on a flat surface.
- In the center of 1 sheet of aluminum foil put ½ cup canned corn.
- On top of the corn, add 1 piece of salmon. Around the salmon put 1 cup of chopped broccoli.
- Using about 2 teaspoons of cajun seasoning, liberally season the salmon and broccoli.
- Cut ½ tablespoon of butter into 4-6 small pieces and dot it among the broccoli. Sprinkle broccoli lightly with salt.
- Repeat with the second piece of salmon.
- Fold the foil packets up to keep juicy and steam inside. Place both packets in the air fryer basket and cook for 15-20 minutes until salmon is 145 F internally or flakey to touch. Broccoli should be fork tender.
- Remove from the foil packets and serve with fresh lime wedges.

Nutrition Facts

- Calories: 142| Protein: 29.7g| Carbohydrates: 1.9g| Fat: 1.1g| Cholesterol : 60.7mg| Sodium: 183.9mg.

41. Air Fryer 'Shrimp Boil' For Two

Prep Time: 10 minutes

Cook Time: 15 minutes

Total Time: 25 minutes

Ingredients

- 3 small red potatoes, sliced 1/2 inch rounds
- 2 ears of corn, cut into thirds
- 1 Lb easy-peel shrimp, defrosted
- 14 Oz smoked sausage, cut into 3-inch pieces
- 2 Tbsp vegetable oil
- 1 Tbsp Old Bay Seasoning

Instructions

- Combine all ingredients in a large bowl and drizzle with oil, Old Bay Seasoning, salt, and pepper. Transfer to the basket attachment of air fryer and place basket on the pan.
- Place in the air fryer and set to the fish setting, toss after 7 minutes.
- Carefully remove and serve.
- Chef's Note: If the potatoes are cut too large they may not finish cooking.

Nutrition Facts

- Calories: 1,250
- Total Fat: 74g
- Saturated Fat: 22g
- Trans Fat: 0.5g
- Cholesterol: 485mg
- Sodium: 3750 mg
- Total Carbohydrate: 74g
- Dietary Fiber: 8g
- Sugars: 10g
- Protein: 72g

42. Air Fryer Garlic Shrimp – Hawaiian Style

Prep Time: 12 minutes

Cook Time: 8 minutes

Total Time: 20 minutes

Ingredients

- 1 pound shrimp, shells-on
- 4 tablespoons ghee (or butter)
- 4 garlic cloves, minced
- 2 tablespoons arrowroot flour/starch
- 1 1/2 teaspoons paprika
- 1 teaspoon salt
- 1/2 teaspoon pepper
- Cooking spray

Instructions

- Clean and devein the shrimp. Pat the shrimp dry as possible.
- In a large bowl, combine the arrowroot flour, paprika, salt, and pepper. Add the shrimp and toss gently. Make sure each shrimp is evenly coated in the flour mixture.
- Line the air fryer with liners. Add shrimp to the air fryer basket in a single layer. Do not stack shrimp. You may

need to cook this in batches depending on how large your air fryer is. Spray the shrimp lightly with cooking spray.

- Set air fryer temperature to 350 degrees. Cook 8 minutes, flipping halfway through. When you flip the shrimp, spray the other side lightly with cooking spray.
- Add ghee to a small saucepan and melt over low heat. Once melted, add garlic and cook 2-3 minutes until the garlic starts to turn a light brown color. Turn off & remove from the heat so you don't burn the garlic.
- Use tongs to remove shrimp from the air fryer. Pour garlic butter mixture evenly across all the shrimp.

Nutritional Value

- Calories: 327| Protein: 33.7g| Carbohydrates: 4g| Fat: 18.5g| Cholesterol: 99.1mg| Sodium: 810.8mg.

43. Air Fryer Fish Nuggets

Prep Time: 10 minutes

Cook Time: 10 minutes

Total Time: 20 minutes

Ingredients

- Two 3oz filets of thick white fish – I used cod
- 1 egg
- 1/2 cup almond flour
- 1 tsp salt
- 1/2 tsp pepper

- 1/2 tsp garlic powder
- 1/2 tsp smoked paprika
- Spray oil

Instructions

- Cut the fillets of fish into bite-size nuggets
- Whisk the egg in a small shallow bowl
- In a separate shallow bowl combine almond flour, salt, pepper, garlic powder, and smoked paprika
- Bread each fish nugget by first dipping in the egg, then coat in the almond flour mixture
- Place each breaded nugget on the air fryer tray
- Spray lightly on all sides with cooking oil – I used spray avocado oil
- Cook in the air fryer at 425F for 10 minutes
- Remove, allow to cool slightly, and enjoy!

Nutrition Facts

- Calories: 337| Protein: 18.8g| Carbohydrates: 16.9g| Fat: 22.9g| Cholesterol: 47mg| Sodium: 920.7mg.

44. Air-Fried Crumbed Fish

Prep Time: 10 mins

Cook Time: 12 mins

Total Time: 22 mins

Ingredient

- 1 cup dry bread crumbs
- ¼ cup vegetable oil
- 4 flounder fillets
- 1 egg, beaten
- 1 lemon, sliced

Instructions

- Preheat an air fryer to 350 degrees F (180 degrees C).
- Mix bread crumbs and oil in a bowl. Stir until the mixture becomes loose and crumbly.
- Dip fish fillets into the egg; shake off any excess. Dip fillets into the bread crumb mixture; coat evenly and fully.
- Lay coated fillets gently in the preheated air fryer. Cook until fish flakes easily with a fork, about 12 minutes. Garnish with lemon slices.

Nutrition Facts

- Calories: 354; Protein: 26.9g| Carbohydrates: 22.5g| Fat: 17.7g| Cholesterol: 106.7mg; Sodium: 308.9mg.

45. Seafood Linguine

Total Time: 35 mins

Servings: 4

Ingredient

- 8 ounces whole-wheat linguine, or spaghetti
- 2 tablespoons extra-virgin olive oil
- 4 cloves garlic, chopped
- 1 tablespoon chopped shallot
- 1 28-ounce can diced tomatoes, drained
- ½ cup white wine
- ½ teaspoon salt
- ¼ teaspoon freshly ground pepper
- 12 littleneck or small cherrystone clams, (about 1 pound), scrubbed
- 8 ounces dry sea scallops
- 8 ounces tilapia, or other flaky white fish, cut into 1-inch strips
- 1 tablespoon chopped fresh marjoram or 1 teaspoon dried, plus more for garnish
- 1/4 cup grated Parmesan cheese, (optional)

Instructions

- Bring a large pot of water to a boil. Add pasta and cook until just tender, 8 to 10 minutes, or according to package directions. Drain and rinse.
- Meanwhile, heat oil in a large skillet over medium heat. Add garlic and shallot and cook, stirring, until beginning to soften, about 1 minute.
- Increase the heat to medium-high. Add tomatoes, wine, salt, and pepper. Bring to a simmer and cook for 1 minute. Add clams, cover, and cook for 2 minutes. Stir in scallops, fish, and marjoram. Cover and cook until the scallops and fish are cooked through and the clams have opened, 3 to 5 minutes more. (Discard any clams that don't open.)
- Spoon the sauce and clams over the pasta and sprinkle with additional marjoram and Parmesan (if using).

Nutrition Facts

- Calories: 460| Protein: 34.5g| Carbohydrates: 55.8g| Dietary Fiber: 8.2g| Sugars: 7.5g| Fat: 9.5g| Saturated Fat: 1.6g| Calcium: 86.5mg| Iron: 4.5mg| Magnesium: 122.1mg| Potassium: 474.9mg| Sodium: 1173.3mg.

46. Seafood Paella With Spring Vegetables

Active Time: 1 hr 15 mins

Total Time: 1 hr 35 mins

Servings: 6

Ingredient

- 6 tablespoons extra-virgin olive oil, divided
- 2 cups diced onion
- 1 cup diced fennel
- 3 medium tomatoes, grated on the large holes of a box grater (skins discarded)

- 4 cloves garlic, thinly sliced
- 2 tablespoons white-wine vinegar
- 1 teaspoon sea salt, divided
- ½ teaspoon ground pepper
- ½ teaspoon crushed red pepper
- Pinch of saffron
- 1 large fresh artichoke
- 1 cup Calasparra rice or other paella rice
- 2 cups seafood stock
- 1 cup green beans, trimmed and cut into 2-inch pieces
- 4 ounces squid bodies, sliced into rings
- 6-12 clams and/or mussels, scrubbed
- 8 ounces skinned monkfish or cod, cut into 1-inch-thick pieces

Instructions

- Heat 3 tablespoons oil in a 13- to 14-inch paella pan over medium-high heat. Add onion and fennel; cook, stirring often, until the onion is translucent, about 5 minutes. Add tomatoes, garlic, vinegar, 1/2 teaspoon salt, pepper, crushed red pepper, and saffron. Reduce heat to maintain a simmer and cook, stirring occasionally, until the tomato liquid has evaporated, 20 to 25 minutes.
- Meanwhile, clean artichoke. Cut lengthwise into 6 wedges. Heat 2 tablespoons oil in a large skillet over

medium heat until very hot but not smoking. Add the artichoke wedges; sprinkle with 1/8 teaspoon salt and cook until browned, about 2 minutes per side. Transfer to a plate.

- Preheat oven to 375 degrees F.
- When the tomato liquid has evaporated, add rice to the paella pan, increase heat to medium, and cook, stirring, for 2 minutes. Add stock. Turn on a second burner so both the front and rear burner on one side of the stove are on; bring to a boil over high heat.
- Spread the rice evenly in the pan and nestle the artichokes and beans into it. Reduce heat to maintain a low simmer and cook for 10 minutes, rotating and shifting the pan around the burners periodically to help the rice cook evenly. Season squid with 1/8 teaspoon salt and place on the rice. Cook, without stirring but continuing to rotate the pan, for 5 minutes more.
- Nestle clams and/or mussels into the rice with the open edges facing up. Season fish with the remaining 1/4 teaspoon salt and place on top of the rice. Remove the paella from the heat and very carefully cover the pan with foil.
- Transfer the pan to the oven and bake for 10 minutes. Let stand, covered, for 10 minutes before serving.

To Prep A Fresh Artichoke:

- Trim 1/2 to 1 inch from the stem end. Peel the stem with a vegetable peeler.
- Trim 1/2 inch off the top.
- Remove the small, tough outer leaves from the stem end and snip all spiky tips from the remaining outer leaves using kitchen shears.
- Cut in half lengthwise and scoop out the fuzzy choke with a melon baller or grapefruit spoon.
- Keep artichokes from browning by rubbing the cut edges with a lemon half or putting them in a large bowl of ice water with lemon juice.

Nutrition Facts

- Calories: 354| Protein: 16.1g| Carbohydrates: 38.2g| Dietary Fiber: 4.7g| Sugars: 5.2g| Fat: 15.3g| Saturated Fat: 2.3g| Calcium: 65.6mg| Iron: 1.7mg| Magnesium: 51.4mg| Potassium: 695.1mg| Sodium: 695.3mg;

47. Spaghetti With Garlic & Clam Sauce

Total Time: 45 mins

Servings: 8

Ingredient

- 2 heads garlic
- 28 fresh littleneck clams, scrubbed and rinsed well
- ¾ cup cold water
- 5 tablespoons extra-virgin olive oil, divided
- 2 tablespoons all-purpose flour
- 1 cup dry white wine, such as Pinot Grigio
- 1 cup chopped fresh parsley plus 2 tablespoons, divided
- 1 tablespoon chopped fresh tarragon
- ¾ teaspoon freshly ground pepper, divided
- 1/8 teaspoon crushed red pepper (optional)
- 1 pound whole-wheat spaghetti or linguine

Instructions

- Put a large pot of water on to boil.
- Peel 1 head of garlic, separate cloves, and halve any large ones. Peel the second head and chop all the cloves.
- Place clams in a Dutch oven or large saucepan with cold water. Cover and cook over high heat, stirring frequently, until the shells just open, 6 to 10 minutes.

Transfer to a bowl as they open, making sure to keep all the juice in the pan. Discard any unopened clams. Reserve 16 whole clams in their shells. Then, working over the pot so you don't lose any of the juice, remove the meat from the remaining clams. Coarsely chop the meat; set aside separately from the whole clams. Pour the clam juice from the pan into a medium bowl, being careful not to include any of the sediment. Rinse and dry the pan.

- Heat 4 tablespoons of oil in the pan over medium heat. Add all the garlic and cook, stirring, for 1 minute. Stir in the chopped clams and cook for 15 seconds. Add flour and cook, stirring, for 15 seconds. Increase heat to high, stir in wine and the reserved clam juice. Bring the sauce to a simmer, stirring constantly to prevent the flour from clumping. Once it's simmering, reduce the heat to medium and stir in 1 cup parsley, tarragon, and 1/2 teaspoon pepper. Cook, stirring often, until slightly thickened, 6 to 8 minutes. Add crushed red pepper, if using. Add the reserved clams in shells and stir to coat with the sauce.

- Meanwhile, cook pasta in boiling water until al dente, 10 to 13 minutes, or according to package directions. Stir 2 tablespoons of the pasta-cooking water into the clam sauce, then drain the pasta and transfer to a large serving dish. Stir the remaining 1 tablespoon oil and 1/4 teaspoon pepper into the pasta. Spoon the clams and sauce over the pasta. Sprinkle with the remaining 2 tablespoons parsley.

Nutrition Facts

- Calories: 371| Protein 17.8g| Carbohydrates 49.6g| Dietary Fiber 7.3g| Sugars 2.5g| Fat 10.3g| Saturated Fat 1.5g| Calcium 83mg| Iron 3.8mg| Magnesium 97mg| Potassium 431.8mg| Sodium 412mg;

48. Air Fryer Coconut Shrimp

Prep Time: 30 mins

Cook Time: 15 mins

Total Time: 45 mins

Ingredient

- ½ cup all-purpose flour
- 1 ½ teaspoon ground black pepper
- 2 large eggs
- ⅔ cup unsweetened flaked coconut
- ⅓ cup panko bread crumbs
- 12 ounces uncooked medium shrimp, peeled and

deveined
- cooking spray
- ½ teaspoon kosher salt, divided
- ¼ cup honey
- ¼ cup lime juice
- 1 serrano chile, thinly sliced
- 2 teaspoons chopped fresh cilantro

Instructions

- Stir together flour and pepper in a shallow dish. Lightly beat eggs in a second shallow dish. Stir together coconut and panko in a third shallow dish. Hold each shrimp by the tail, dredge in flour mixture, and shake off excess. Then dip floured shrimp in egg, and allow any excess to drip off. Finally, dredge in coconut mixture, pressing to adhere. Place on a plate. Coat shrimp well with cooking spray.
- Preheat air fryer to 400 degrees F (200 degrees C). Place 1/2 the shrimp in the air fryer and cook for about 3 minutes. Turn shrimp over and continue cooking until golden, about 3 minutes more. Season with 1/4 teaspoon salt. Repeat with remaining shrimp.
- Meanwhile, whisk together honey, lime juice, and serrano chile in a small bowl for the dip.
- Sprinkle fried shrimp with cilantro and serve with dip.

Nutrition Facts

- Calories: 236; Protein 13.8g; Carbohydrates 27.6g; Fat 9.1g; Cholesterol 147.1mg; Sodium 316.4mg.

49. Air-Fried Shrimp

Prep Time: 5 mins

Cook Time: 10 mins

Total Time: 15 mins

Servings: 4

Ingredient

- 1 tablespoon butter, melted
- 1 teaspoon lemon juice
- ½ teaspoon garlic granules
- ⅛ teaspoon salt
- 1 pound large shrimp - peeled, deveined, and tails removed
- Perforated parchment paper
- ⅛ cup freshly grated parmesan cheese

Instructions

- Place melted butter in a medium bowl. Mix in lemon juice, garlic granules, and salt. Add shrimp and toss to coat.
- Line air fryer basket with perforated parchment paper. Place shrimp in the air fryer basket and sprinkle with Parmesan cheese.
- Cook shrimp in the air fryer at 400 degrees F (200

degrees C) until shrimp are bright pink on the outside and the meat is opaque for about 8 minutes.

Nutrition Facts

- Calories: 125; Protein 19.6g; Carbohydrates 0.5g; Fat 4.6g; Cholesterol 182.4mg; Sodium 329.7mg.

50. Garlic Parmesan Air Fried Shrimp Recipe

Prep Time: 5 Minutes

Cook Time: 10 Minutes

Total Time: 15 Minutes

Ingredients

- 1lb shrimp, deveined and peeled (you can leave tails on if desired)
- 1 tbsp olive oil
- 1 tsp salt
- 1 tsp fresh cracked pepper

- 1 tbsp lemon juice
- 6 cloves garlic, diced
- 1/2 cup grated parmesan cheese
- 1/4 cup diced cilantro or parsley, to garnish (optional)

Instructions

- In a large bowl, add shrimp and coat in olive oil and lemon juice, season with salt and pepper, and garlic.
- Cover with plastic wrap and refrigerate for 1-3 hours. (Optional, for more lemon flavor.)
- Toss parmesan cheese into the bowl with shrimp, creating a "breading" for the shrimp.
- Preheat air fryer.
- Set air fryer to 350 for 10 minutes, add shrimp to the basket and cook.
- Shrimp is done when it is opaque white and pink.
- Serve immediately.

Nutrition Information

- Calories: 151
- Total Fat: 6g
- Saturated Fat: 2g
- Trans Fat: 0g
- Unsaturated Fat: 3g
- Cholesterol: 167mg

51. Air Fryer Garlic Shrimp With Lemon

Prep Time: 5 mins

Cook Time: 10 mins

Total Time: 15 mins

Ingredients

- 1 pound (454 g) raw shrimp, peeled deveined,
- Vegetable oil or spray, to coat shrimp
- 1/4 teaspoon (1.25 ml) garlic powder
- Salt, to taste
- Black pepper, to taste
- Lemon wedges
- Minced parsley and/or chili flakes (optional)

Instructions

- In a bowl, toss the shrimp with the oil or spray to coat. Add garlic powder, salt, and pepper, and toss to evenly coat the shrimp.
- Add shrimp to the air fryer basket in a single layer.
- Air Fry at 400°F for about 8-14 minutes, gently shaking and flipping the shrimp over halfway through cooking. Cooking times will vary depending on the size of shrimp and on different air fryer brands and styles.
- Transfer shrimp to the bowl, squeeze lemon juice on top. Sprinkle parsley and/or chili flakes and serve hot.

Nutrition Value

- Calories: 164kcal | Carbohydrates: 1g | Protein: 31g | Fat: 3g | Saturated Fat: 1g | Cholesterol: 381mg | Sodium: 1175mg | Potassium: 121mg | Sugar: 1g | Vitamin C: 6mg | Calcium: 219mg | Iron: 3mg

52. Shrimp Poke

Active Time: 30 mins

Total Time: 30 mins

Servings: 4

Ingredient

- ¾ cup thinly sliced scallion greens
- ¼ cup reduced-sodium tamari
- 1 ½ tablespoons mirin
- 1 ½ tablespoon toasted (dark) sesame oil
- 1 tablespoon white sesame seeds
- 2 teaspoons grated fresh ginger

- ½ teaspoon crushed red pepper (Optional)
- 12 ounces cooked shrimp, cut into 1/2-inch pieces
- 2 cups cooked brown rice
- 2 tablespoons rice vinegar
- 2 cups sliced cherry tomatoes
- 2 cups diced avocado
- ¼ cup chopped cilantro
- ¼ cup toasted black sesame seeds

Instructions

- Whisk scallion greens, tamari, mirin, oil, white sesame seeds, ginger, and crushed red pepper, if using, in a medium bowl. Set aside 2 tablespoons of the sauce in a small bowl. Add shrimp to the sauce in the medium bowl and gently toss to coat.
- Combine rice and vinegar in a large bowl. Divide among 4 bowls and top each with 3/4 cup shrimp, 1/2 cup each tomato and avocado, and 1 tablespoon each cilantro and black sesame seeds. Drizzle with the reserved sauce and serve.

Nutrition Facts

- Calories: 460; Protein 28.9g; Carbohydrates 40.2g; Dietary Fiber 9.9g; Sugars 4.5g; Fat 22.1g; Saturated Fat 3.2g;; Calcium 113.2mg; Iron 3.2mg; Magnesium 145.1mg; Potassium 939.3mg; Sodium 860.6mg.

53. Air Fryer Fish Sticks

Prep Time: 10 mins

Cook Time: 10 mins

Total Time: 20 mins

Ingredient

- 1 pound cod fillets
- ¼ cup all-purpose flour
- 1 egg
- ½ cup panko bread crumbs
- ¼ cup grated parmesan cheese

- 1 tablespoon parsley flakes
- 1 teaspoon paprika
- ½ teaspoon black pepper
- Cooking spray

Instructions

- Preheat an air fryer to 400 degrees F (200 degrees C).
- Pat fish dry with paper towels and cut into 1x3-inch sticks.
- Place flour in a shallow dish. Beat egg in a separate shallow dish. Combine panko, Parmesan cheese, parsley, paprika, and pepper in a third shallow dish.
- Coat each fish stick in flour, then dip in beaten egg, and finally coat in seasoned panko mixture.
- Spray the basket of the air fryer with nonstick cooking spray. Arrange 1/2 the sticks in the basket, making sure none are touching. Spray the top of each stick with cooking spray.
- Cook in the preheated air fryer for 5 minutes. Flip fish sticks and cook for an additional 5 minutes. Repeat with remaining fish sticks.

Nutrition Facts

- Calories: 200; Protein 26.3g; Carbohydrates 16.5g; Fat 4.1g; Cholesterol 92.5mg; Sodium 245mg.

54. Air Fryer Cajun Shrimp Dinner

Prep Time: 10 Mins

Cook Time: 20 Mins

Total Time: 30 Mins

Ingredients

- 1 tablespoon Cajun or Creole seasoning
- 24 (1 pound) cleaned and peeled extra-jumbo shrimp
- 6 ounces fully cooked Turkey/Chicken Andouille sausage or kielbasa*, sliced
- 1 medium zucchini, 8 ounces, sliced into 1/4-inch thick half-moons

- 1 medium yellow squash, 8 ounces, sliced into 1/4-inch thick half-moons
- 1 large red bell pepper, seeded and cut into thin 1-inch pieces
- 1/4 teaspoon kosher salt
- 2 tablespoons olive oil

Instructions

- In a large bowl, combine the Cajun seasoning and shrimp, toss to coat.
- Add the sausage, zucchini, squash, bell peppers, and salt, and toss with the oil.
- Preheat the air fryer to 400F.
- In 2 batches (for smaller baskets), transfer the shrimp and vegetables to the air fryer basket and cook for 8 minutes, shaking the basket 2 to 3 times.
- Set aside, repeat with remaining shrimp and veggies.
- Once both batches are cooked, return the first batch to the air fryer and cook for 1 minute.

Nutritional Value

- Calories: 284kcal| Carbohydrates: 8g| Protein: 31g| Fat: 14g| Saturated Fat: 2g| Cholesterol: 205mg| Sodium: 1500mg| Fiber: 2g| Sugar: 3g

55. Air Fried Shrimp With Garlic & Butter

Prep Time: 5 mins

Cook Time: 6 mins

Total Time: 12 mins

Ingredients

- 3 tbsp butter (or ghee) melted
- 3 cloves garlic minced or pressed
- 12 XL shrimp 16/20 or smaller
- 1 tsp sea salt
- 1 tsp freshly ground black pepper

Instructions

- Wash the shrimp in cold water. If needed, using kitchen shears, slit the top of the shrimps and devein. Keep the shells on and place the shrimp in a medium bowl.
- Turn on the air fryer to preheat to 360°F
- In a small bowl, mix the melted butter or ghee, and garlic.
- Pour the garlic and ghee mixture over the shrimp to marinate.
- Place the shrimp in the air fryer basket. Set the timer to 6 minutes.
- Reserve butter and garlic mixture for later.

- When the timer goes off, open the basket and check for doneness. If the color of the shrimps is red and the flesh is opaque white, they are cooked. These shrimps were XL and it only took 6 minutes. Depending on the size, the cooking time may vary.
- Place the shrimps back in the medium bowl and toss them with the reserved garlic butter mixture.
- Sprinkle sea salt and black pepper and toss well. Serve immediately.

Nutrition

- Calories: 106.2kcal | Carbohydrates: 1.1g | Protein: 0.8g | Fat: 11.3g | Saturated Fat: 7g | Cholesterol: 36.4mg | Sodium: 605.4mg | Potassium: 9mg | Fiber: 0.1g | Sugar: 0.1g | Vitamin C: 0.7mg | Calcium: 8.4mg | Iron: 0.1mg

56. Zesty Ranch Air Fryer Fish Fillets

Prep Time: 5 minutes

Cook Time: 12 minutes

Total Time: 17 minutes

Ingredients

- 3/4 cup bread crumbs or Panko or crushed cornflakes
- 1 30g packet dry ranch-style dressing mix
- 2 1/2 tablespoons vegetable oil
- 2 eggs beaten
- 4 tilapia salmon or other fish fillets

- Lemon wedges to garnish

Instructions

- Preheat your air fryer to 180 degrees C.
- Mix the panko/breadcrumbs and the ranch dressing mix. Add in the oil and keep stirring until the mixture becomes loose and crumbly.
- Dip the fish fillets into the egg, letting the excess drip off.
- Dip the fish fillets into the crumb mixture, making sure to coat them evenly and thoroughly.
- Place into your air fryer carefully.
- Cook for 12-13 minutes, depending on the thickness of the fillets.
- Remove and serve. Squeeze the lemon wedges over the fish if desired.

Nutrition Information

- Calories: 315kcal| Carbohydrates: 8g| Protein: 38g| Fat: 14g| Saturated Fat: 8g| Cholesterol: 166mg| Sodium: 220mg| Potassium: 565mg| Calcium: 50mg| Iron: 1.9mg

57. Easy Air Fryer Shrimp & Vegetables

Prep Time: 15 minutes

Cook Time: 15 minutes

Total Time: 30 minutes

Ingredients

- 1 pound thawed shrimp (about 21-25), peeled, deveined and tails removed
- 1 red bell pepper, cut into 1-inch chunks
- 1/2 yellow onion, cut into 1-inch chunks
- 1 tablespoon avocado oil or olive oil
- 1 teaspoon chili powder
- 1/2 teaspoon garlic powder
- 1/8 teaspoon cayenne pepper (a small pinch!)
- 1/2 teaspoon salt
- 1/2 teaspoon fresh ground black pepper
- **Optional To Serve:** Rice, quinoa, pad thai noodles, more veggies, teriyaki sauce, etc

Instructions

- **Prep:** Thaw and remove the tails from the shrimp. You can cook them tails on but I like to get it over with so I can enjoy my meal tail-free. Place the shrimp in a strainer to remove the excess liquid. If you're serving with rice, start that now. Make sure the veggies are prepped and ready to go.

- **Mix it:** Add the shrimp, bell pepper, onion, oil, chili powder, garlic powder, cayenne pepper, salt & black pepper to a medium-sized mixing bowl and stir to combine.
- **Cook:** Place seasoned shrimp and vegetable mixture into your air fryer basket. Set the air fryer to about 330F degrees (my air fryer is analog so it's not exact). Air fry the shrimp and vegetables for 10-13 minutes total, shaking the basket halfway through.
- **Serve:** Serve with rice, quinoa, pad thai noodles, or any other carb you prefer. Store leftovers in an airtight container for up to 4 days.

Nutrition

- Calories: 362 Fat: 7g Carbohydrates: 50g Fiber: 4g Protein: 43g

58. Air Fryer Fish Sticks

Prep Time: 15 minutes

Cook Time: 10 minutes

Total Time: 25 minutes

Ingredients

- 1 lb cod filet
- 1/4 cup all-purpose flour
- 1 large egg
- 1 cup Panko breadcrumbs
- 1/2 tsp garlic powder

- 1/4 tsp dried parsley
- 1/4 tsp onion powder
- 1/4 tsp salt

Instructions

- Preheat the air fryer at 400 degrees F for 10 minutes.
- Meanwhile, cut the cod into approximately 1" sticks.
- Place the flour into one shallow bowl.
- Place the egg into one shallow bowl, and whisk.
- Place the panko, garlic powder, parsley, onion powder, and salt into a separate shallow bowl, and stir to combine.
- Dip each fish stick first into the flour, then into the egg, and finally in the Panko breadcrumb mix, making sure you completely cover at each step.
- Spray the air fryer with cooking spray and place half of the fish sticks into the basket.
- Cook at 400 degrees F for 5 minutes, flip, and then cook another 4-5 minutes, depending on the thickness of your fish sticks.
- Serve with tartar sauce and enjoy!

Nutrition

- Calories: 405kcal | Carbohydrates: 34g | Protein: 50g | Fat: 6g | Saturated Fat: 2g | Cholesterol: 203mg | Sodium: 674mg | Potassium: 1035mg | Fiber: 2g |

59. Air Fryer Fish And Chips Healthy

Total Time: 20 Minutes

Ingredients

- 4-6 oz Tilapia Filets
- 2 tablespoons of flour
- 1 egg
- 1/2 cup of panko bread crumbs
- Old Bay Seasoning
- Salt and pepper
- Frozen Crinkle Cut Fries such as Ore Ida

Instructions

- Gather 3 small bowls. In one bowl add the flour, in the 2nd bowl add the egg and beat it with a wire whisk, in the 3rd bowl add the panko bread crumbs and Old Bay Seasoning.
- Take the fish and dredge it in the flour, then the egg, and next in the bread crumbs. Add to the air fryer along with 15 frozen french fries. Air Fry for 15 minutes at 390 degrees.
- Serving size: 1 tilapia filet. Use serving size on fry package for fries and measure out accordingly.

Nutrition

- Calories: 219| Sugar: 1g| Sodium: 356mg| Fat: 5g| Saturated Fat: 3g| Carbohydrates: 18g| Fiber: 1g| Protein: 25g